THE MALADIES OF THE LAMPS

for my wife, Claudia-Doina.
and our son, Cosmin -Leonard

GEORGE VULTURESCU

English Version: *Olimpia Iacob & Jim Kacian*

ISBN: 978-93-88319-75-1

First Edition: 2021
Rs. 200/-

Cyberwit.net
HIG 45 Kaushambi Kunj, Kalindipuram
Allahabad - 211011 (U.P.) India
http://www.cyberwit.net
Tel: +(91) 9415091004
E-mail: info@cyberwit.net

Printed at Thomson Press India Limited.

Contents

1. THE THREE-IN-THE-MORNING POEM 5

THE THREE-IN-THE-MORNING POEM 6

THE SANDALS OF THE POET LAUREATE 8

I DID NOT THINK I WOULD LEARN. 10

THE POET WHO LUGS HIS LINES WITH THE ELEPHANTS 13

THE METAPHYSICS OF THE EMPTY SACK 15

POEM WITHOUT A MIDWIFE 17

THE ROOF OF THE HOUSE AND THE TITLE OF THE BOOK 19

A FOOL REQUIRES A KING 21

ULYSSES PAYS FOR HIS VOYAGE IN BANKNOTES
WITH THE IMAGE OF BRÂNCUȘI 22

HAVE YOU EVER CRIED OUT, "A STONE HAS COME BACK TO LIFE"? 24

THE SUNDAY OF MY FEAR 26

ECCLESIASTES EFFECT 28

THE GRAMMAR OF SHADOWS 30

THE MAGUS WITH THE TWIG OF A HAZELNUT TREE 32

A POET DOES NOT PAY HIS LETTER AS A WHORE 33

A FISH SWIMS IN YOUR EYE 35

GAUGUIN ATTACHES A BAYONET TO HIS BRUSH 37

THE BOARD OF THE RAFT 38

THE BOARD OF THE RAFT 39

BENEATH THE HOOF 40

2.DISCREET AS SOMEONE 43

CALLED TO THE MORGUE TO IDENTIFY A CORPSE 43

RAMBLINGS OVER A GAME WITH IGITUR 44

THAT MARINE GIANT FISH WITH YOUR HARPOONS. 45
WHAT MISTLETOE ABSORBS FROM THE TRUNK OF THE TREE 47
ONE SOLE EYE AND ONE SOLE LOOK 48
WE ARE NEARLY LAMPS 49
THE MALADIES OF THE POEM UNDER THE LAMP 52
BY A WATTLE FENCE 54
WOMEN SURROUNDED BY FLAMES 56
EVEN THE BREATH OF A DYING MAN CAN SUPPORT A WING 58
A COCK FOR ASCLEPIUS 60
THE NORTH IS IN THE SOUND OF THE STONE 62
LAMPS' POEM 64
IS "THE STARRY SKY" VISIBLE AT THE AUTOPSY? 66
THE WORDS AND THE HORSESHOES ON THE DUSTY ROADS 68
THE SNAIL IN THE POEM 70
TO THE BONE 71
POETRY'S SWADDLING CLOTHES 74
DISCREET AS SOMEONE CALLED TO THE MORGUE TO IDENTIFY A CORPSE . 76
3. PROVINCIAL JOURNAL 79
ILLUSIONS TO LIGHT THE LAMP 80

1. THE THREE-IN-THE-MORNING POEM

THE THREE-IN-THE-MORNING POEM

Every time I write
the three-in-the-morning poem
my hands become useless
the stumps push them with their blood
as high floods push the mud over the fields

The three-in-the-morning poem
sits at the table with the living and the dead
it wanders in the heavy rain with Vallejo
one Thursday through Paris
near a street lamp it tries to loosen
the tie of Gerard de Nerval,
on a dissection table it sees
a sewing machine and
an umbrella
it tries to open the oven of Sylvia Plath
it listens to the ores that miscarry crystals
as clays crack making room for
the roots of narcissi
the letters of the three-in-the-morning poem are also made out of clay
you would spit on them just as the Maker has done
when He made us from clay
letters are mild clay
before you burn them in the three-in-the-morning
furnaces

Nothing is for gods at three o'clock in the morning
wolves know the way to the beds and howl at the moon

the owl knows and sings on the shed
you psalmodize with Reiner Maria Rilke:
he who wanders goes to himself
he who dies in the night sees himself
Death makes room for the three-in-the-morning
poem
he recognizes in it the letters made of clay
he recognizes in them the earth of your grave
only with the eyes of the poem you can look at death

though one of your eyes is Blind and the other Healthy,
do not make him poor:
let the morning's embers be seen
in the hollows of your eyes
as wolves see the glowing embers
in the hearths of the houses
you know that the malefactors in the North
do not come with lamps
they come in the light of the glowing embers in the knife blade
wolves howl at the moon
the owl sings on the houses
winds dissipate the dust from the graves

only the clay of the three-in-the-morning poem
sieves from one letter into another
as the she-wolf keeps her cubs safe
carrying them in her mouth
from one gorge to another

THE SANDALS OF THE POET LAUREATE

I sing about your sandals, poetry.
Some people say that they weigh 99 okas iron and 99 okas steel.
They are what I need to come back
under the cross. Borges, the Argentine, wondered
if then your thought had run to the kingdom
that awaited you in the skies or
to a woman that was not yours.
Now Golgotha is deserted, Nazarene,

In the marketplace the poets recite psalms about Your wounds.
Their sandals are immaculate.
They sell spears at the newsstands – souvenirs–
like the centurion's that has pierced your ribs.

I come in to have a vodka. Someone keeps preaching between the tables:
"He, the Resurrected One, has risen up into the sky. Do you think it was fair
that He should continue to stay with us on earth
waiting for Jeanne d'Arc, crusades and the long row of martyrs?. . ."
Someone else answers:
" I have been a rottenness of a fungus. . . When you hit the stone
with the flint steel, you need sawdust, fungus, dry straw
to catch the spark for the fire. . ."

In the outside roar they confer diplomas,
crowns of laurels.
I come out with your sandals, poetry:

some people say that they weigh 99 okas iron and 99 okas steel.
I wander wearing them to the poppy flower in the field.
No spear shall wound for your blood red, poppy flower.
Has anyone seen blood on the sandals
of the poet laureate?

I DID NOT THINK I WOULD LEARN. . .

1.

To wander through the cobalt woods
of a lamp
in search of the little hazel twig of the poem
you need a Blind Eye and a Healthy one:
The Blind Eye keeps the lightning's ashes
the Healthy one gazes as the blood does.

The glow worms say,
"Cold does not come from the poets who wander
like some lamps through the fog,
as death, also, does not come from the dead—
it is the very hour when all powers are active:
earth, air, water and fire. . ."

Now the Blind Eye comes into the Healthy Eye,
it sinks and comes to rule over its black,
or blue or green pupil.
The Healthy Eye always remains dislocated
outside the Blind Eye—
as resin does outside the tree bark .

It is not a good thing for you to have a Blind Eye and
a Healthy one:
no one feels safe around you
until they find out what you see;
it is not a good thing for you to speak about a North
where maladies are in a lamp—
where God increases the tallow and the green bees

that come out from the flames' honeycombs to dissipate the fog.

2.

The lamp, like memory,
has slow spreads of hemp balls,
of whirls and muddy weeds,
through which the drowned look for your hands when you write.
Do you swim for them or write for yourself?

The glow worms say,
"Like the fetus in a mother's womb, the poem
does not let itself be taken from under the lamp. . ."

No one dies if a poet wanders through the fog—
But we are not safe until we know
if the fog in which he writes
is the same as the fog between the striations
in our brains;

No one dies because a blind man has lost
the light of his eye,
one dies because we fail to know what he sees:
no one dies if the little hazel twig in the poems
is cold as a sword,
or warm as the neck under the guillotine,
but we are not safe until we know
if it still performs any magic. . .

3.

It is not a good thing for you to speak about the North
where there are blind lamps,

many blind lamps so many
that the way to the North no longer goes North

But the glow worms say to me,
" The poems with lamps fail to show us the way,
they only remember it to us. . ."

THE POET WHO LUGS HIS LINES WITH THE ELEPHANTS

They heard louder and louder the elephants' tramping
approach the city
the governors on the payroll shook
like a spider's web in the wind

What were they bringing with the elephants on that day,
the poets of the provinces,
who never sit at the table
with the distributors of ribbons?

Strangers came into the sumptuous halls
and displayed the pages of their poems
just as go-betweens unfolded the mantles
on the bodies of the slaves for sale in markets.
They suddenly saw their own lines
through the eyes of the people present
they heard their words lashing their ears
and began to like them —
they had had genius on that very dark night of the province
where she-wolves look for embers in the fires left unguarded—
now, there, in front of them, they know that for them
they will refuse all the money in the world

Fools they must have been, the poets of the provinces,
to come to the fairs on that day
they, who never sit at the table with the distributors of
ribbons—
fools, also, my elephants who knew

that you could bind a bargain only for your own weight
fools because they leisurely put my poems, line by line,
on the spider's web of the silence in the hall
where the governors on the payroll continued to swing
still expecting gold, myrrh, and frankincense
but only a crazy poet from the North
still has elephants
to go with him wherever he wants

THE METAPHYSICS OF THE EMPTY SACK

I have never written psalms—
 it seems to me that a psalm is like warm bread
 you have to take to the poor

How could I deliver it? How long could I stand, gasping,
carrying on my shoulders the sacks of lines turned into bread
in the huts among the rocks,
and the hovels, and the street corners?

And if I happened to come across thieves, Sodomites
or king killers—how could I make the right choice?

You think of Jesus who has never surrendered to temptation, saying:
"Man shall not live by bread alone"
but we continue to tread on stones
groping between the warm bread, the earthy one", and
"the bread in the skies" of the chosen—
one is eaten here, with a hot mouth, made of flesh,
as the other one, only when your lips
become clay and ashes.

But I cannot say it, who has chosen me
to say it to those who snatch the bread out
of my hand, scratching me, biting me.
The Jesus in the text about the loaves of bread is sad for them,
and also for me, who stretch out my hands towards him asking him
to make them be of stone, so that I may no longer be bitten.

It is “a shit of metaphysics”, you say
after Dostoievsky,
and leave the poem as before
a “way between nothing and nothing”
as Jesus, too, has left stones to be stones,
not having turned them into loaves of bread

You, happy ones, would you keep coming to the poem
only for the metaphysics of the empty sack?

POEM WITHOUT A MIDWIFE

You are always in a new line— God's ear
for tomorrow's bread—
on today's crumbs from the bread we have been given
are seated the heralds in wait for a Thursday with heavy rain
the black heralds come only when you have supper
all by yourself with today's poem

you have no midwife for it— you encourage yourself following a Frenchman's advice
who has written about afternoons with fauns:
"the poem comes into being all by itself".
I wonder if your life is or is not a crumb of another line
as Jesus also is only in the apostles' epistles

In a poem with a midwife Ecclesiastes writes for you
you may have supper with apostles
and may multiply bread and wine
but you do not know what you will write about in tomorrow's line
for which you eat today's bread
as a midwife also does not know whether the fetus will have
two heads joined directly to each other
or harelips

This makes me grumble:
no one speaks about crumbs
at the Last Supper
no one speaks about the other hand

that passes on the scribe's name of the coryphaei of the Academy
no one knows whether he who will carve your name on the
wooden cross
is born

You have no midwife at the birth of today's poem—
your hands remove the blood from it and cut
Its umbilical cord—
for a while letters frisk through the brain's striations
like lambs on pastures, with downcast eyes
and awkwardly bent necks
before the claws of vultures and wolves
ready to snatch them from among the weeds

now you have blood on the page—
blood never comes back into the wound
nor letters into the milky muds of night
in the brain
a midwife can wash away the fetus' blood from her hands
you cannot bring together round today's poem
twelve apostles or twelve beggars
in the street
Vallejo's heralds alone are nearby
at any moment they can bring together twelve mild people,
twelve apostles,
twelve thieves
and lie in ambush to see how you tremble among the letters
as if in a sinister forest that grows up around you
with every word of tomorrow's poem

THE ROOF OF THE HOUSE AND THE TITLE OF THE BOOK

Make your book as a "turn-key" house
on the Ozana bank or the Some' River
with languishing rooms, and a porch
and a tiled roof.

You passed through barracks, boarding schools and prisons
(how many years?) to a gentle fire in the violet room
where you roll the woman's body
on the white, yet so green, bedsheet
breast to breast, tooth upon tooth—
two knives peeling the apple of this poem.

How long can you—thoughtless as the crow on the branch,
be a poet "coal burner" —screwed up among the books,
among the oak panelling on the walls
only plagiarizing their death watch?

It is the hour when you remember:
Jesus said to the paralytic, "Pick up your pallet and walk!"
Somewhere, shining, buzzing— terraces,
rooms and halls hosting ill-famed recitals.

If chrysalises could come out
from the silk case of your poems
how many words would still want to remain but as larvae
under the dictatorship of the "masterpiece" of the book?

It is the hour when you know that you get the title
before every line in the book
that the roof of the house walls has been finished
when the best roof a house can dream of
is the snowstorm, is it?

isn’t that the real masterpiece?

A FOOL REQUIRES A KING

You see him:
he, who awkwardly bears my white cane along the streets
of an old town on the Some' River, is not a fool.

Now he ricochets it off an iron coin—
there are hidden forces that work to raise the coin
from the dust on the road.
The angels look from the moss on the walls:
"Will he kneel before the arms and the king's image stamped on its side?
"He could be the pedestrian dying under his pennants
without having taken the pay for his mother in the village. . ."

There are hidden forces in the coins on the roads—
there are moles of ruined coats of arms
and white ants that feed the fool's fear
that the king will fail to recognize himself in his laughter.
That's what they have in mind when they see how he bends
and picks up the coin. He wipes it
with his palm, steams it with his warm breath,
and then comes into the bar.
He throws it on the counter for a glass of alcohol
A royal eagle rises from the drawing of the arms and shadows the hall.

One person sees it. Maybe two.
The barman turns the coin on both sides
but there is no inscription on it.
He laughs, stirring the customers:
" Who lends a king's image
for this coin?. . ."

ULYSSES PAYS FOR HIS VOYAGE IN BANKNOTES WITH THE IMAGE OF BRÂNCUȘI

The Prince is a fool:
he drinks the most expensive wine and holds on his knees
the most yearned-for whores of the fair
the barman does not accept his gold coins
with worn-away coats of arms left on the counter

from the corner table (where I keep writing, awaiting
Buck Mulligan)
I offer myself to pay in his place
with banknotes on which is the portrait of Brâncuşi
gone from town long ago
that spiral, James Joyce, he drew for you
in Montparnasse, *relativement tel que moi*,
is but a sign of fear
of looking at each other, *le sens du pousser*
along the streets that have never been trodden by princes

"Fear is a cage", added the Prince
without turning toward me.
I have just paid for you, I'm about **to cry out**
but the soldiers ask me questions about the coins
with worn- away coats of arms that have not been included
in the Monetary Nomenclature in the
town.

"Yes, I've seen him", I declare to them. But I never know
where and when I could meet him. I was *at Finnegans*

Wake and I heard him crying out:
Go out for a minute, Lazarus! The Last Judgement!

There is no Prince in town, the soldiers kept making a fool of me.
Time for you to go home: the barman was no longer angry with you
because you had spoken to him about his mother's death,
the female students who had been accosted at the bar
withdrew their actions
because you had told them about
Caliban's rage who could not find his image in the mirrors

I went out, walking along the streets with my self, somehow
squashed. I waved to the taxi driver
and gave him a banknote with the portrait of Brâncuşi.

"Are you sure, Mister Bloom, that the cutters
in the woods speak in the pubs about
the rings of *mysterious growth* in tree trunks ?. . ."

He turns toward me and I recognize him in the dull image of the Prince
on the gold coins.
"The spiral is great freedom: it borrows
the invisible right from God". So spoke
the Prince. I also was there . . .

HAVE YOU EVER CRIED OUT, "A STONE HAS COME BACK TO LIFE"?

Let foolishness envelop them
as mothers' swaddling clothes in their cradles
let them have memories—
from a wheat field
from a lawn of narcissi
from a street in New York where they heard the chime bells
on a sleigh from the Oa' county
they have not yet read Langston Hughes' line,
"What will become of us
in front of
what we remember . . ."

You come out from the poem as if from a bathtub—
the soap suds with the flesh's dirt slip along the pipes of the outlet canals:
you cut your nails
raze your beard
detach the dry crust from the wounds left by daggers
stealthily stabbed between your shoulder blades

neither thrown away on the bank like a fish,
nor fallen from a swallow's nest
or left near the door of the monastery as a whore's baby
or with a torn sandal
or a button pulled out from shirt sleeves
or an iron spur broken from the boots

was there a field of magnolia?
were there pieces of rubbish from the huts taken away by
the waters?
was there a stench coming from the swamps?

Move away when you have no proof
you have neither drizzle in your hair
nor mud on your patent-leather shoes
or hard flesh in your palms because of spades
In a line you've stared at yourself, seeing your face all wrinkles,
boils, quite deformed as if by a funhouse mirror.
In another line you've boiled and dyed eggs red
to tap them against other people's on Easter Night — "Christ
has risen!"
but the birds in their yolks will never fly
—birds do not bring red eggs to churches
nor babies through house chimneys —
In the past you struck two stones together
and saw the spark springing from their sarcophagus
but you've never cried out, "A stone has come back to life
through a spark !"

The poem's foolishness envelops you
as in the cradle your mother's swaddling clothes
and you cannot ask,
is stone the poorer without spark?

THE SUNDAY OF MY FEAR

It is a whore of an evening in the North
that lowers its veils over your eyes
as daggers leave scars through the town's corners.
This is what you do on the Sunday of your fear in the North
you stay with a whore of a book—
reading is a brothel

"The queen mates and dies.
Is the beehive only for the words-little bees
that make candle wax, which is pleasant for churches?"

That's what I ask old Bards on the Sunday of my fear
In the North
which feeds on the defamation of the hieroglyphs from other books.
They, all, are stingy, good at definitions:
"The poem has its glory and the poet his death . . .
You are not in a nest on its page where the stork
brings frogs in its maw from swamps for its young . . ."

You see much better when the knife blade sparkles,
sliding along another knife,
than on the Sunday of your fear when you cannot find
your writing paper. You make torches of the pages
of other books about fear—
their ashes fall upon your white sheet of paper
like an urn emptied out in an ossuary
you no longer know which speck of dust was a tibia,
which one a heart's aorta, which one the ear's lobe.
It is the Sunday of your fear in the middle of the page

a whore of a fear that follows you every night in the North
when you can say to ashes,
"Brother Borges,
Brother Eminescu,
Brother Kafka,
what burns, does it "continue to dream" the blow of the winds?

Ash is now the page on which you write
on which you would like to write
but in ash specks of dust fail to line up
as planets in the skies
instead they gather up "with neither rhyme nor reason"
as the whore's words
in the ear of your fear in the North

You find no stone on which to carve a letter
not even wood good for a cross on which
to scratch a name
the pieces of wood crouch in the acorn of clay
and the hatchet is there
on the structural frame of the brain's clearness
patient whore's clearness
the hatchet is there every evening
and your fear on its handle
like a king's hand that waves to the fool
to laugh in his place

who would hesitate near this whore of a hatchet
on a night of fear in the middle of the pages? . . .

ECCLESIASTES EFFECT

Fool that I am, a victim of belles-lettres,
I go out along the bank of the Some' River and listen to its waters:
"Ecclesiastes and I are the same age —
I have dug the river bed myself.
Above my waves
the wind alone blows as it likes.
On your page, poet, is there a bigger snowstorm?"

That makes me think twice:
"I can give names to the stones that dash
against the wall of the Zothmar city under the weight
of the stones above
I write the letters myself with which I ask Ecclesiastes:
'what comes after ashes, what do they turn into?'
'what comes after the wind, what does it sweep away?'"

Meanwhile in the bushes on the bank of the Some' River
the wolf's little muzzle seeks the she-wolf's breast
this summer the waters of the Some' River have dried up:
here and there are muddy water holes
with little fish struggling
I've seen a child carrying a bucket
to bring them water from the tap of his block of flats.
Fish have no Ecclesiastes to tell them
that "all streams flow into the sea, yet the sea is never full".(1)

At the end of the bridge a beggar awaits
a coin, mumbling:
"No poet will be born in Sãtmar;

many will come here only to die
and many more will leave soon
to find death somewhere else . . ."

If you are a poet, that makes you think twice:
is a beggar needed on a bridge in a province town
or only the wind?

I do not give him any coin:
I go with it into the first bar
where if you come once, you will like to come again
and if you have a drink you will like to have it again
and if you write at a table, you will write again —
the poem does not deviate from Ecclesiastes —
every poem is good to be the last
every town is good for you to die in
or leave it soon so that you may find death
somewhere else

*1) Ecclesiastes, ch. 1:7 ("All streams flow into the sea, yet the sea is never full. To the place the streams come from, there they return again.)

THE GRAMMAR OF SHADOWS

I am one of the poets who has seen the wolves face to face—
through the thick young woods of Sãlaj shadows are red:
shadows peel your eyes' thin skin
and you see the wolves with the blood
and you know that inside you are not dead

There are embers round me at night when I write
you are not blind if you see embers—
they keep the flame in their glow
as wolves keep their claws in their sheaths
as stones they walk on keep their sparks
in their cold cores
writing removes the skin on words
I write with their very steamy memory
memory is the claw that feeds my poem

You hear only their howling
descending on the membrane of your ears
as caterpillars on leaves
there is no national howl
to guarantee community rights
and I am not a Marx-Engels of wolves
nor does my poem stand for their bushes

In the moon's kratophany I watch over the words' embers —
yes, there are days when I run over the stones of the sly hours
with wolf's paws springing at the sheep's neck —
dull it stays in the grass believing that God has made it
graze without cease the young shoots on the hillocks:

sheep do not have a Mother Teresa to guide them,
wolves do not intonate psalms in the ravines,
their access is direct: their bite

Not even on the page, where you are, "the good keeper"
of the words — sheep, the grammar of wilderness is not different:
underwood all of a heap, trees' divisions,
separation of leaves

He who has seen a wolf face to face
knows that in his eye sockets are but embers
the flame grows strong only in its spring
you write by their embers, in the cold's grammar between
one word and another
you see red between the words — sheep
you see right with the blood between the words — wolves
and you know that you are not dead inside you

THE MAGUS WITH THE TWIG OF A HAZELNUT TREE

Does the black of letters ever bloom?
They say that Poetry takes out from the ashes
the pattern of the rose with Paracelsus' hand

Every letter flickers. It burns my fingers.
Your body, mother Irina,
your body, father Gheorghe,
rise for a moment from the ashes of memory,
as you pick up the seeds in the tub full of wheat,
scattering them.

I am a scatterer of ashes.
I am a scatterer of letters
as the drummer's fingers meet just for a moment
the tumult of sounds on the drum skin
If only I could find their silence
as I found it in the evening when you told me the story
about the little twig of a hazelnut tree.

I am a scatterer of ashes, mother,
as in a cave is silence on the page
to the right of our land was Father Achim's
to the left was Toader's
the silence on the page has nothing to the right
and nothing to the left
every line is a twig of coal
in the morning I have a shaft of ashes

the magus, what was he saying, mother?

A POET DOES NOT PAY HIS LETTER AS A WHORE

I kept hunting a shadow, or a woman:
so low did I go down your streets that night
oh, Sãtmar!
The linden trees had shed their blossoms:
there was but the smell of a palisade of twigs
cut off from the swamps of the Some' River
steaming among the boards and from the passages.

Heavy with the poison of the glasses, my blood
kept pulsing in my temples. My body grew thinner
by the flagstones of the streets as the shivs
on the rubbing stones: I could hunt anything at that hour.
There was no angel in the streets,
no owl. The dry oils of the letters
on the walls began detaching
just like shells and were crushed underfoot
I came down to fear's hogwash, where
drunkards' vomit flows
where cigarette butts
are sticky ashes under soles.

"I am looking for you", I said to the Whore.
"All want to have you: they come from afar
and they pay you in coins of gold
Is your bed a fold
or a forest for hunting?"

I kept hunting a shadow, or a woman:
So low did I go down your streets that night
o, Sãtmar!
Both poetry and "doughy flesh " are in the folds—
when I write I do not arrange the letters in the word
as a whore in a bed.
There must be a heretical letter
that could turn Death's eyes from you,
as mirrors can turn the ray of light . . .

"A poet does not pay his letter as a whore",
whispered the voice in the Night to me.
"The stag is by the spring,
the whore's body in the alcove.
Sometimes, near the dead bodies, the poem is
like a coin left for the grave diggers . . ."

A FISH SWIMS IN YOUR EYE

Motto:

Is it that **death forgets** to free.
You fishes of melancholy?
(Apollinaire)

Fish do not exist for the river water
neither does the river exist for fish
but the big fish—that wants to swallow
the small fish, what does it know?

God is a fish in your right eye,
that's what you find out, looking at the Some' River.
You are allowed to carry it as the river
carries the fish to the sea.

Day by day you please it with violet blue,
you feed it on the mist enveloping the willows,
on the steams of the muds in the swamps,
on the stalks of the weeds between the clods and the stones.

It moves its little wings through the cornea and pupil
up to the border of the retina—and from there bam!
It springs into another eye
that looks at you from among the others.

"They do not know who was the first
to carry it in his eye, through the town", laughs someone in the street.
Does God not try to descend
in the hell of every soul?

The river does not run dry because it takes
the fish away to the sea.
Your body, with the river of blood and flesh,
will it die because day by day it feeds
the fish without death?

I won't make the river be more beautiful,
lying that fish exist only for it
I will not lie saying either that my eye
is a drop God swims in
as the sky mirrors itself in a drop of dew.

Go away, river, go far away, I say to you,
what is the use of my bearing out the beauty
of the fish that has swum through my eye
if blindness alone could prove it?

GAUGUIN ATTACHES A BAYONET TO HIS BRUSH

So tired, so tired
that you dragged yourself to reach your room.
You did not even notice the body of the Polynesian girl, Tehura,
lying in bed. [

You see it when you paint the scene:
through the background of the canvas
the eyes of a woman, embers rotting in them,
keep screwing.

Now you recognize Tehura —
You see her well of flesh gushing out
Before the night of forms:
"The line never sleeps, it is but
the spark from the glowing embers . . ."
Now you would like to attach a bayonet to your brush
as soldiers to their weapons
to keep guard* over the place where death comes into the painting:
"The painting is not a vat
In which you plunge your ladle, as often as you wish,
for a helping of the imaginary . . ."

* The Spirit of the Dead Watching " the title of a painting of Gauguin, dating from 1892. An engraving (1890-1894) has a similar title, " SHE THINKS OF THE SPIRIT OF THE DEAD"

THE BOARD OF THE RAFT

Don't say to me that you cannot bathe twice
In the same river
one thousand drops bathe in the river
one thousand drops bathe in the sea

on the page you are only once
on its raft
scratched by one thousand drops
wandering upon the tops of one thousand waves

You are hungry and thirsty
you have nothing to eat, nothing to drink on the page
you cut off one finger from your hand
you cut slices of your shank and of your breast
and up to the bank the hand that writes cuts off
the other hand that holds the page

O, God, don't say that the poem
is the board of the raft
the last one, out of which you can bite!

THE BOARD OF THE RAFT

Don't say to me that you cannot bathe twice
In the same river
one thousand drops bathe in the river
one thousand drops bathe in the sea

on the page you are only once
on its raft
scratched by one thousand drops
wandering upon the tops of one thousand waves

You are hungry and thirsty
you have nothing to eat, nothing to drink on the page
you cut off one finger from your hand
you cut slices of your shank and of your breast
and up to the bank the hand that writes cuts off
the other hand that holds the page

O, God, don't say that the poem
is the board of the raft
the last one, out of which you can bite!

BENEATH THE HOOF

Fear is a hoof
fear is an ivory tower
in your ivory tower it gets warm as in an igloo
the ivory castle grows bigger when you write about
the ivory tower
as if you wrote with clay adobe
as if you wrote with river stones
as if you wrote with scales when you are afraid
on your page
there is no square
nor a circle of chalk
there is no merit in the calligraphy
fear's hoof leaves when it pulls down
the ivory towers of the canonical poets
there is no merit when the poem grows
within the ivory castle
as if the hoof grew within
fear's scales

One day you see that fear alone remains on the tower
with its iron feathers, with metallic claws
like a black raven that looks into the far distance
stuck on the ramparts of your poet
like a hoof in the river silt

When the hoof comes down upon the nest in the grass
you cannot philosophize about the bird in the yolk of the egg
nor about the ant on the way to its mole
there is no calligraphy in the lines

the hoof leaves
nor in your brain's stria
—all is but gruel under your brain pan when you write —
whence rats full of epistemological fetuses come out
and gnaw the hoof's scales that keep them in the words
of the poem

In the middle of your text there is always a hoof
that squashes your line
descends into your liver, your bowels,
examines your organs one after another and croaks within them
as every wall of the ivory tower
cracks and falls down,
as the completed line falls down into the line not completed yet

only graves would tread so heavily
over the world if they began
to walk with the dead's bones;
they alone could say to us whether one could reach the sky
from beneath the hoof
or whether one could ascend with hoof's scales alone

2.DISCREET AS SOMEONE

CALLED TO THE MORGUE TO IDENTIFY A CORPSE

RAMBLINGS OVER A GAME WITH IGITUR

Motto: "*I was the hour which is to make me pure*"
(Mallarmé— "Midnight")

"When I do not throw them on the board
the dice come nearer, all alone,
and slide over one another —
could you believe that chance has one minute of delicacy? . . ."

"Do letters promise more? Sometimes
they do not care about the poem and remain on the white page,
they glide innocently — as wrecks sink
out at sea — ones to others."

"It means that you can rely on the ones
that crept like snakes, the ones that went
to lure you into the wild
when Jesus did not change stones into bread . . ."

"Are they a promise? The barren fig tree,
does it enlarge the wild or is the anxious eye
of the lonely one who arrives hungry,
under its branches? . . ."

"I throw letters, Igitur, not dice,
I throw letters at the Hawk that watches over the line,
the blind Hawk, which does not turn the page
and leaves the end without end . . ."

THAT MARINE GIANT FISH WITH YOUR HARPOONS. . .

I have put out the gas lamp in the room —
an intense halo has replaced the flame for a while
like a fissure in the dark

I am happy that the night is not a tree hollow
in the core of the tree
happy that the night has no alembics and retorts
but our veins
happy that the night has no bowels
its bowels do not rumble
in my writing every letter rumbles
you do not know whether it does not leave tree hollows in words
as the void in the storks of the reeds

what does the letter assume together with us, Novalis?

A Christ hangs on the wall of a central pub
in which I sit over a glass of vodka
his eyes seem to look like the mesh of a net
cast over the waters by boatmen
I hear Saint Ciprian among the customers:
"Extra ecclesium nulla salus . . ."
I believe
that there is no night beyond night
the art of fissure begins when letters do not come back to the poem
when every letter becomes a harpoon
you have impaled the giant fish of poetry

The night withdraws from my brain
as fog from moors
brain is but a moor full of brackish water
in which the big-bellied letters croak

A fisherman lifts the empty net on the water
you lift the bed sheet from your lover's body

Far off, in the offing, that marine animal
struggling with all your harpoons.

WHAT MISTLETOE ABSORBS FROM THE TRUNK OF THE TREE

There, where wolves suck their wounds and
bear their young in their mouths to another lair
there, where pike spawn
in the silt from under the willows
there, on the rocks, where vultures mate,
in the killers' nightmares when they sense the iron of the shiv
glide along the bone

God is late a moment

storks bear living things in their craws and leave them in the nests
to feed their young
until they fling themselves over the edge
into the hollow of the air

what can you take away from a nest?
from the she-wolf's lair in the thick young wood?
from the cocoon of the silkworm
what does the butterfly carry?

this is what poetry bears:
what mistletoe absorbs from the trunk of the tree.

ONE SOLE EYE AND ONE SOLE LOOK

It is right to be so: I cannot always recognize myself
in the mirror, in the eyes of the people around.

The strength to ignore your own line marked with chalk
and the strength to pass through its dust
with your boots
gives you the prestige of the one thousand eyes
that open in every letter of the poem

To be in all letters makes you feel dizzy
their hunger makes you feel dizzy
and also the pages full of dead letters and living letters —
I do not always recognize myself in living things
I cannot look straight into the eyes of dead ones
as I cannot simultaneously look
at the one thousand leaves under which lies the nest

The lightning alone simultaneously sees
the tree
with its one thousand leaves
and also the nest on the branch.
This is what I read in Maistre Eckhart:
*"my eye and God's eye are
one sole eye and one sole look"*

And when my eyes close under death's eyelids
what does God see together with me?
And what do letters and I simultaneously see?

WE ARE NEARLY LAMPS

"If someone has changed us into moles", says Ion,
"This evening's fog smells of bandages on wounds",
adds Alexandru
"It runs on my skin as a rope round the neck
of a hanged man", I render justice to him

It is cold in the Province when you look for a pub,
along the streets, in a town on the Some' River,
where eroticism solely in pigeons' cooing
urges on life

They, those poets in the night,
are not good examples for the Academy,
because cold does not come from the poets who wander
through the fog,
as death also does not come from the dead.
They do not wander in the cold "pro patria", but "fool about"
from a "bloody imperative of authenticity"
which makes you come out in the night
from the tomb of a book, coming to life,
to the tomb of another
only for you to finish the poem begun under the stuffy rays
of a lamp that has ravaged your eye
under another lamp, a purplish-blue one, in the pub of Humã
the light of which you intensify with your own eyes
looking for it through the fog.

"We are nearly lamps", cries out Ion, "ever since
we have walked on through the fog . . ."

Do you know that in the painting "The Last Supper" there are
no lamps? broke out Alexandru.
"I definitely know", add I, "that no one has changed us into moles,
if we can look at the painting of Leonardo . . ."

Izidor, the pub musician, sings in a drawling voice:
"*There is no light anywhere . . .*"
I decide to tell him that what he says is similar to the answer
The Crucified One gives the children in "The Dream" of Jean Paul:
"*Jesus, do we have a Father?*"
We, all, are orphans", He says.
But Izidor comes to our table and confesses himself,
clinking the glasses:
"Above me a Musician, who is Greater than Me,
sings. I hear His words turn into icicles . . . "
Then he laughs, turning to Ion, the poet:
"Have you ever seen The Great Line from above
your line . . . ?"

In my dream it is the gas lamp hanging from
the wooden beam in the house
of Tireac. I am seated at the table with my father and my sister,
Maria. Mother brings in knot-shaped breads and warm milk for us.
If we gathered up all the lamps from the houses of our childhoods,
wouldn't death turn blind, unable to find
the way to us?

Somewhere, at a table, under the ecumenical lamp of the pub,
a voice asks:
"When the Pope prays, how many lamps are there around him . . . ?"
But Izidor starts singing again:
"*Nowhere there is light . . .* "
"Someone, perhaps, has changed us into moles", murmurs Ion.

"Cold, perhaps, does not come from the poets who wander through the fog,
as death, also, does not come from the dead . . ."

THE MALADIES OF THE POEM UNDER THE LAMP

1.

There are nights when the light of the lamp makes me as small
as a well-off bug in the pages of Kafka;
there are nights when the light of the lamp crushes me
as the hoof flattens the soft clay —
it makes me and my writing one
as, in the cell, the monk and his prayer are one.

I am not what you want, God,
I am not the tallow in the lamp, nor the cloth wick
that burns,
I do not fall at the feet of darkness
as the lightning's ashes fall
after the fir has been burnt

I struggle under the lamp like a fish on a hook:
is it not you who have cast the fishing line?

2.

"You do not become an angel if you pray under the lamp,
but if you know to put it on in your soul you will",
said to me my mother Irina.
There were nights when I felt it flicker
in my fears—
A lamp inside another lamp —
I protected its flame with my ribs

and it moved through my bowels
as a fish through the pool.

3.

A woman pressed her face to my face,
her mouth to my mouth,
as you press your face to the lamp shade
when the cold in the room seizes you
the lines of her body clung to me like the lashes of a switch
Do I burn? Is the light of the lamp flagellation?
Let winds scatter my ashes
up to the sky, God.

4.

There were nights when the shadows cast by the lamp
ran dry in my brain as some creeping stalks.
I shall set them on fire, I said to myself,
because it is always cold in a brain haunted by shadows.
"They are your memories", glow worms cried out to me,
You will no longer know who you have been . . ."

I thought that the lamp drives idols away,
but it drove me away from home and
I wandered in the night to the first pub:
"Turn the light higher, host", I cried out,
to recognize the coats of arms on the coins
with which I want to pay all the devils here! . . ."
"In my pub of the North, the light in the knife blade
is enough for you to recognize
the coats of arms on the coins . . ."

BY A WATTLE FENCE

I am not intimate with collectors
but I think taxes should be introduced among letters

unpunished I pass among their columns
unpunished I write among them with saws bursting into flames
under wolves' eyes
from under the cornea of my eye
What do they do there in my brain's thick young wood
in which I have never been able to enter?

Scratched letters lie on my pages
like some pools of blood.
Later you find out — blood cannot come back
Into the wound. And you, stone of diamond, polished with lasers,
Would you come back into the bowels of the rocks
in the necklace round Marilyn Monroe's neck?

Unpunished, I choose a form of letter:
round as the ones in the ABC book, coiled up and
winding from Arabian borders: others are slippery
as the icicles hanging from the stack eaves,
some are soft — similar to silk ropes which
spiders hesitate to climb
others sharp as the stakes around which we
weave the sticks to make fences

this is what I see now — a wattle fence in a village
a child passing it by with a little knapsack round his neck —
on its linen there are two firs

and a stag with a star on its brow. Has he come out to go from home to home singing Christmas carols? Or does he bear a round of bread to a sick grandmother?

He does not know yet — he will live among letters
as others are fated to sleep on pillows embroidered
in golden thread:
if you do not go to the North, the North will not even exist,
child. You are not welcome with a little knapsack
in the garden full of golden apples

You have stirred the lightning bolts
even an ordinary poet in the province
may find himself under lightning bolts
if he wears a little knapsack round his neck

in a garden full of golden apples,
who will come back after he has looked at them
through a wattle fence?

WOMEN SURROUNDED BY FLAMES

The Vulture's eyes see the small insect in the grass,
others, close to us, remain unclear.

This allegory was given to me
by a stranger on the Some' River bridge:
she,leaning against the guard rail, did not see me.
I had just left in a room
a women's warm and naked body on the bedsheet:
we, both, had carried much water to the mill
to tear to rags and tatters innumerable nights
as two cogged wheels upon the shaft that moves
the grinding stones

I went out on tiptoe and felt
the scales grow on my soles . . .
I ran away (there are no laws to condemn the abandoning of a woman's naked body in a warm bed)
the girl on the bridge did not see my hooves grow
while I was running
if she had turned to me, she would have screamed,
If she had screamed, my scales would have flown to bits,
(the memories' slaughter occurs in "a lighted hall
with walls made of mirrors", you read in Mihai Eminescu)

The Vulture's eyes see dust and powder
I did not see the ice floes on the river,
nor the transparent ones that froze in the girl's eyes,
I saw only the flames around her
"I see every woman surrounded by flames —

the flames in a nuptial bed are a circle
defending us from death

May the Vulture's eyes see dust and ashes,
may the lighted hall with walls made of mirrors
go to hell,
may it go to hell if it does not burn
like a nuptial bedsheet!

The poem that does not sense the Vulture's claw
on its lamb's back,
does not deserve to be finished.

EVEN THE BREATH OF A DYING MAN CAN SUPPORT A WING . . .

I saw many people who wished for wings,
buying cages,
my eyes were in tears when I saw
cages
I was happy that my eye sockets had
no gratings to stop my tears
I wished only Old Achim's White Horse
(he would give it to me only to take it by the bridle
to the water trough of the draw well).
"When you hear it speak, it will be yours,"
he teased me waggishly.

I wore a Blind Eye and a Healthy Eye
among the villagers
but not even a child wished to thrust his finger
into the hollow eye socket of my Blind Eye
to touch the muddy skin of
"the creatures in the lairs".
"You have to let yourself be haunted by darkness,
to see", Old Achim advised me.

After his death they took the White Horse
to the slaughterhouse in town.
Ever since then it has come every night
when I write, through the dilated galleries
of my Blind Eye:
it takes me among the viscous storks of shadows,
among angels with lamps in which green bees
distinguish the dead from the living.

I have seen swallows flying a thousands times
to bring in their beaks blades of grass and thin creeping stalks
which they stick under the eaves
with argillaceous clays.
My Healthy Eye knows that the white page
has no gratings such as cages have —
nor is my Healthy Eye a cage:
through its niches there are not scratched
the damned's traces of nails —
the walls of its galleries are made of black diamond
and nails glide like sledge runners.

The White Horse carries me night by night
when I write:
Arabian green hieroglyphs detach themselves from
the cities' frontons to join me
as if some clusters of dolphins.
Old Achim's White Horse is now mine,
it speaks to me every night:
"Do not choose the lines as you engage your carters;
the poem is not a flying carpet . . ."

I do not know the number of Blind Eyes birds fly through
at this hour in the world
I do not know the kind of air that supports their wings

"Flying is possible", Old Achim said to me,

"even the breath of a dying man
can support a wing to a nest . . ."

You did not know that it is within you
and can support you
as ice flowers support your glance
in frost's drawings on the window.

A COCK FOR ASCLEPIUS

When I write, Row comes to me and
waggishly whispers pranks over my shoulder.
He could sit on the arabesque of the letters as on a branch,
light as it is, and throw little pebbles
on the surface of my poem:

"Shakespeare was *a co-operative society"*, says
Montale to us: "he used charlatans
as full of genius as he was"1 Why do you keep clear
of the part I add to your lines?

"*I would prefer not to*", I feel like crying out at him as
Bartleby and Co., but the charlatan within me
refrains from it — he knows that you will find out:
the poem begins somewhere else, where I am proud of Row
(without wishing to be Row) because he is able to come back
after the lost sheep — a letter quite scared that urinated
behind another bush of letters. . .

At some other time there are whole nights
when Row does not appear near me when I write
I call him from the middle of *a bad line*
that noisily detaches itself as ice floes
on the rivers in springtime. I desperately wave my hand:
but only as I fathom *the good line* I reach the bank,
the bad line crushes against the other ice floes,
rattling among the piers of the bridge . . .

I struggle not to be Row, I drink poison
in his place but he wanders among the young woods
to look for healing herbs for me. "Let us stop separating
the good one from the bad one . . .", he cries out at me,
Let me go, what will your Name be"2,
I throw it in his face. The blood of the wounds
is enough for me — let it ooze! Without it we are
lighter than angels . . .

"*An angel on credit*", continues Row,
appropriating from Celine's text.
But I know that Row exists only if my eyes,
pious as they are, see him among the stalks of the letters
come and bring me the Nurofen tablet
from the drugstore.

"Mind the great Asclepius says that you have not sent him
a rooster", he says to me while I swallow the pill
with a mouthful of water.

I am fine:
may I be forgiven for the death of the cock but
I have to feed *the good line*
may I be forgiven for *the bad line, too,*
because it alone makes the good line come alive . . .

1. See the poem: " *Literary histories*", **in Quadermo di Quattro anni**, Milano, 1977
2. *Genesis*, Ch.32, 26, 27

THE NORTH IS IN THE SOUND OF THE STONE

1.

Smother your fear: stones do not attack

Titir no longer watches over his poor pasture:
he roams the fairs in a golden coach,
Holding the beauty on his knees
no one watches over the hubbub of stones:
they bleed, crouch, crumble under the others' weight

2.

My eye's look despoils all the hillock of the North —
the green of the herbage
and the leaves and the stalks' miasmas —
I do not choose to believe anyone:
transcendence is a flow of substance
between my Healthy Eye and my Blind Eye
it swims like a fish through the stone
ichthyologists do not know what to believe

3.

Only the stones of the North held me on their knees:
I saw Poetry on the clayish roads
of the province, in the lashing drizzle
in the shepherds' huts, on the paths and ravines with
lumberjacks, on the side of the road with go-betweens and
carvers of crosses, on the backstreets with the imperial and royal
soldiers of the city of Zothmar

4.

Alexia, beside me, was naked in the grass
when the storm began,
the lightning burned the fir tree nearby
The Blind Eye asked,
"Do lightning bolts die when they burn wood?"
The Healthy Eye also asked,
"Do lightning bolts continue to die like the dead
after they have become ashes?"

5.

The Province has no knees to rock you, child

On the hillside there is a cliff ground by hard frosts
Wind, in a whirlwind raise my sand again
over the hills
The North's Virtue is making you feel the stone's great pains
supporting the sky.

LAMPS' POEM

My Blind Eye and my Healthy Eye
talk about lamps, mother,

"A green light dances in the lamp's flame
like a mad woman locked up and abandoned in an asylum room.
Green is her braid and also the walls
out of which blades of grass spring

When I write, Midnight allures me
with this mad woman locked up in the lamp's glass . . ."

"There is no green light
but lamps dancing in the green fog
as women dance naked in the grass
on the hills on Sânziene Night*.
With their dance they entice your line
at Midnight
There is no beauty greater
than when the Black Venus comes out
from the black waters of the eye, and chooses you
as white water lilies choose to rise from lake silts . . ."

There is no fear when you write, mother,
whether I look at letters with my Healthy Eye,
or see them in the green fog of the page with my Blind Eye
as I clearly saw before me the two dead man, mother,
that walked beside me in a street of Oa',
while moving their knives in the wind: "Do not rush,
do not jostle because one day the living will kill one another and
there will be more and more dead men . . ."

My Blind Eye and my Healthy Eye
talk about lamps —
a word can dance on my white sheet of paper
like a mad woman locked in an abandoned asylum room
a word can come green before you
or on all fours, in the thirteenth hour
and you will welcome it next to the one
you have had since the first day and placed it in front of the poem

Such is Midnight when you cannot write it:
green, mother, green
and I cannot see you any more, I cannot see you
with my Healthy Eye or my Blind Eye

Note

* *Sânziene Night (June 23rd to June 24th) is considered a mystical moment, when the nature is at its peak and displays its most vital force. The traditional belief is that miracles can happen during Sânziene night, when the skies can open.*

IS "THE STARRY SKY" VISIBLE AT THE AUTOPSY?

You have corrupted my writing, Old Poets,
with the image of that scar of the "starry sky",
with flowers of evil and black agates,
which, once putrefied, turn into drinks
prophesying ashes

Do you think that winds can reign over ashes,
and death gets tired within us and remains
in our tumefied flesh
as virginal the mole's eyes remain under the clays?

But our language is amorous
and manages to enchain our bodies in
Klimt's painting, "Death and Life",
from the Leopold Museum

bodies that start it all over again, day by day, the pains
of being entwined under "the starry sky"
where not even a god has returned any more
as the blood spot cannot come back
to the wound left by the knife

Only one night in a blood spot,
could you still offer the poem, Old Poets,
under the clumsy image of "the starry sky",
where we adulated one another as if in front of a mirror

Was I more than a mole, believing that
“the starry sky” from above
its clay galleries
are our boots’ traces?

In your books, Old Poets,
the autopsy of the enchained bodies in Klimt’s painting,
was done long ago —
is the image of the “starry sky
adorned in the gruel of our brain?

THE WORDS AND THE HORSESHOES ON THE DUSTY ROADS

Goodness knows what I have written lately,
I talk with Row in the Scriptorium.
It is good if he knows, he consents.
The devil will remind you of every line
as if you had given it to him —
he knows why he keeps them
as if you paid with them the whore in him.

The devil is clever —
he gathers up all the good lines and gives them on credit
to other poets left without talent.
All those lines you had hesitated on, you wrote them
trembling, holding the sheet of paper on your knees.
The devil is always present:
he likes the way you work, and rack your brains.

A line the devil has kept
comes back to you when you do not even expect it:
as a dead man lifted from the tomb —
not even you believe that it is yours.

The devil dislikes the grave
and stands on the steps of the Academy.
Scholars recognize him and greets him decently:
Wise minds, he says to them,
it is a line that has slipped through my fingers —
it is dangerous, don't quote it anywhere . . . "

I quickly copy the rebellious line and I place it in the poem
as father quickly nailed the horseshoes
upon the horses' hooves

God laughs from Balzac's mirror:
"a horseshoe does give meaning to the road . . . "
The devil stands at the crossroads, on the other side of the mirror,
but does not know if he gathers up the dead horses' horseshoes
or only the horseshoes badly beaten
on the hooves of the living horses.

In the Scriptorium, Row writes:
"There are no horseshoes for letters —
the poem receives every letter alike
as road dust receives
the horses' lost horseshoes "

Aye, aye,
winds alone can see simultaneously
both the road and the specks of dust on the road.

THE SNAIL IN THE POEM

Aye, belladonna grows fat among the bushes—
there are spoons and knives on the stalls
by road margins
What can you see, what can't I see?

I selfishly see my Blind Eye
and my Healthy Eye tear themselves away
from my brain grown blurred and roaming

One is the whore of shadows with whom
he spends time in dens and galleries.
When it comes back, it brings me fingernails and scales so that
I may swim in the day's puddles
The other brings me tomes of Homilies from the church garrets
in which all letters detach themselves , coming to life like Jesus
leaving the pages blank: *"des Satanes en herbe"*.

That the eye is "a wolf to a man", is not new to me;
That God may be a hoof trace
over the nests in the grass, I have seen;

How little we know about whether letters are "satanical",
as Baudelaire says, or only
"little devils in the grass" —
how little I know about whether one eye may be
healthier than another—
how well I am prepared for the end of a poem
in which letters would come out from the text
—as the snail from its shell—
and would give me "the entrance ticket" back?

TO THE BONE

It was nearly sunset and the Owl
began to see
I nearly sang or wrote

"Among those who touch bottom,
among those who eat the partridge
to the bone
I,tired, await Midnight's Owl.
Why aren't letters stones
so that I may cast them after it?
People should bear a stone
and use it in case of need

Eat Darkness, you, too, kill its black
insects, Owl, you which appear only at sunset;
you eat or you are eaten
I sing after Steven Wilson from *To the Bone*:
there are people around us
who "eat darkness"

Does Darkness have a *bone* — for you to gnaw,
I ask my Blind Eye

But when you come out from the page, there is no one near you,
neither the sentry, nor the apostles;
the poem has remained behind you
as Jesus' shroud in the empty tomb
the holy myrrh bearers will come and see the letters

stained with blood
and you pray to be forgiven for comparison

"Save me from bad lines, God,
lines-Lazarus
that come out from the poem as frogs after rain
and reach the knees of criticism;
lines-the pixie of lakes
which you see only when you throw yourself to the marsh bottom
lines-the fish knows me . . ."

You eat or you are eaten
life can be wounded *to the bone*
that's what I sing with the province poets in the pubs
on the bank of the Some' River
You, Owl, which appears only at sunset,
what do you eat *to the bone,* what do you drink to bottom,
the bone does not gnaw its flesh, says Ion Baias,
the gum does not grind its teeth, murmurs Alexandru Pintescu,
the corn's stalk does not grind its ears, adds
Dorin Sãlãjan

It is nearly morning in the pubs on the bank of the Some' River
The Owl no longer begins seeing us
We, too, no longer see one another
I will take you to the nest, I promise the Owl,
To the Bone, sings Steven Wilson
I will take you to the nests in our tired brain
I will take you to the nests in poets' tired brains —
are you not the mother of all lines?
don't you take them to the nests, the insects of the nightmares

I have nearly reached the eaves of the nest
it nearly looks like the edge of the sheet of paper on which I write
I have nearly reached the bank
the waters of the Some' River reach my ankles
my knees, sings Ion Baias,
my waist, sings Alexandru Pintescu,too,
my neck, sings Dorin Sãlãjan, too

my . . .

POETRY'S SWADDLING CLOTHES

You do not give orders, poetry,
nor does the lightning call out to us to look at it,
nor does death spur us to be born

But my hands curl up against every letter
trying to take you out from the greasy whiteness of the page
as if I took out from the reeds on the bank of the Nile
that wicker basket
in which a baby kept whining

When I write, mother, I am still in
the swaddling clothes in that basket abandoned on the waters —
I hear that the Nile does not call the pharaohs
to the bank to acclaim them
I still do not know whether there are banks at the page margins
its whiteness begets fever vertigoes
they call no one to venerate them —
fever bears all mothers' names,
all the royal signs of the embroideries
on the swaddling clothes of the abandoned babies

It is fog on the banks, mother,
The Nile makes the wicker basket swing
with Moses, the baby, in it,
and the whiteness of the page rocks us as a wet nurse does
letters are the fever's swaddling clothes in which night rocks us

I am fine in poetry's swaddling clothes, mother,
the whiteness of the page cannot be negotiated

by letters
nor even more fruitful
or longer than the Nile
it is the ashes of my name's letters

who will call me by name from the bank?

DISCREET AS SOMEONE CALLED TO THE MORGUE TO IDENTIFY A CORPSE

After a while you will say,
"this poem is not mine",
as if you had been called to the morgue
to identify a corpse.

Summer and autumn sifted over it —
on the Stones of the North she-wolves gave birth to cubs
and took them in their mouths through the ravines
of letters to my door.
Now you are mine, wolves,
I howl like you, I see like you:
who says that you, writing, write about you?

I look with all the rottenness
of the pitch blackness in my Blind Eye
(pitch blackness does not rot, nor does it develop maggots,
pitch blackness does not wonder if in it both the living
and the dead teem)
I look with all the embers in my Healthy Eye:
"This poem is not mine!"
Beauty would not hold it on its knees
I should have a lie for beauty
a lie withstands hymns, Rimbaud,
hell doesn't:
should we accept the starched teachers
with white collars, who dissect and dig beneath letters?
Their criticism on the text of the poem,
is it not like curettages on a woman's uterus?

Should we have a lie for the chicks which
break with their beaks the shell from within the eggs?

After a while you will ask yourself whether the words
of that person who identifies a corpse at the morgue
might belong to a poem
two words
or one thousand words
stretched out like a shroud on the corpse of truth.
Nightmares cannot tear to pieces the thin skin of the eye
as the beaks of chicks break the shell only from within
the egg
if you are not dead you cannot come to life
if you are not alive you cannot write
which part of the shroud are you:
are you the one who raises it?
or the one who is wrapped in it?

Praise be to the holy myrrh bearers
who woke up in the morning!
Praise be to Him whose blood remained
on the whiteness of the shroud and left the Tomb Empty!
Praise be the one from above the page —
is it not as hard for him
as it is rolling away the entrance stone?

He sees the letters stained with blood
but does not deny the corpse:
without a corpse you cannot come back to life
he who holds beauty on his knees holds a corpse
he who tells the truth dissects not only the viscera
of a corpse, but his memory, also.
You are always as discreet in the poem
as is someone called to the morgue to identify a corpse.

3. PROVINCIAL JOURNAL

ILLUSIONS TO LIGHT THE LAMP

"Mankind, naked and mute, with thousands of lamps bewilders us, and Silence continues to be mercilessly oppressive . . ."
(G.M. Hopkins-*Nondum*)

1. I do not look at the light of the lamp, I see with its light.

2. The lamp in my village, like the Star of Bethlehem, is the only one, showing me the way home.

3. We have no weapons to fight against Night, except for armies of lamps.

4. In the tavern, lamps produce illusions: remedies for "the contemporary extreme" — the madness of lamps.

5.What else is left for a man wandering through the fog if not becoming a lamp?

6. Does the lamp light when you take off your dress, or is it alone its lamp shade?

7. Those who stand under the lamp do not see the lamps . . .
Eminescu's Dyonisus says to us: *I shall light my lamp and look for people . . .*

8. The lamp can do a starry sky of the blinded soul.

9. In our stack, in Tireac, under the light of a carbide lamp, father slaughtered a calf for Easter.
If I write about what I see, do I smudge what is under the lamp?

10. For those who do not want to drive away from the light of the lamp, their shadows alone get longer farther away from them.

11. Do you keep the lamp on to see your angel, or do you want him to see you?

12.The gallery you dig in the dark up to the lamp is your light.

13. The lamp accomplishes nothing: *it consumes its fuel.* But it is an insurgent: it is passed on to someone else ahead.

14.The light of a lamp may be "turned yellow", but never patched . . .

15. *"A little light, like a rush light*", sees E. Dickinson. But is it not enough for you to have the feeling that darkness allows a fissure?

16. By a line from Kafka" — *The lamp broke, and a stranger came in with a new light* — I ponder or wait: what can be new: the lamp or its light?

17. Could a people of lamps *"see its soul"*?

18. The lamp does not know the way, but its light helps us see what is on the way.

19. The letters written under the rays of the lamp give irisations as frescos in the Paleolithic caves.

20.Compared to the offering-light of the lamp, writing is frivolous: it can be interrupted, wiped away and done over again . . . But the light of the lamp burns steadily, consuming its oil without any trace of vanity . . .

21. Are you the master of the lamp? You think you can say to it, "Burn in my place, I shall change the wick and the oil to put down suitable letters on the page . . ."

22. Should you "Let your thoughts dwell on the lamp" (J. Brodski) or pay attention to the letters you round under its flicker? If "the letter brings death, and ghost gives life" (St. Pavel, Corinthians 3:6), which shall we oppose: the letter, or the "ghost of the lamp"?

23. With the help of the lampions, I find the way to brothels, under the street lamps I quarrel with the vagabonds, under the light of the lamp I pray like a monk in the cell. And when I pour the tallow into the rushlight, I see the naked body of Tehura, a Polynesian girl, whispering to me, "**The Spirit of the Dead Watching** . . ."

24. The lamp seems to me to be unsuitable not so much for seeing as for confessing about light. That's why I believe it is more suitable for the cells in monasteries . . .

25. Writing accompanies the light of the lamp as shadow accompanies man.

26. I do not call you to come under the lamp, where I, too, cannot remove from writing the weeds that cast shadows as those of letters. So I say to you: the shadow of the lamp can be "corrupted" — it can evangelize shadows. Oppose the lamp to see how your eyes put forth buds in the flesh . . .

Biographical Notes On the Poet

He was born on the 1st of March, 1951, at Tireac, a hamlet in Satu Mare county. He graduated from the Faculty of Philology of the „Babeş-Bolyai" University in Cluj-Napoca. He worked for the culture authority in Satu Mare: the Bookshop Department, the „G. M. Zamfirescu" House of Culture of Satu Mare (as an instructor and then a manager). He was the director of the Department for Culture and National Heritage in Satu Mare county. He is a member of the Writers' Union of Romania – the Cluj branch - and of the Romanian PEN-Club. He has received the Cultural Merit Order, cathegory A, in literature, having the rank of officer. He is a Doctor in Contemporary Literature (2010). He is currently retired.

He is the founder and editor-in-chief of the literary review ***„Poesis"***, Satu Mare (since 1990 up to the present). The review was awarded several prizes (The Writers' Union of Romania and the Romanian Association of the Literary Reviews and the Romanian Publishing Houses). He is the organizer of the International Poetry Festival „Cultural Days – **The Poesis Frontier**", Satu Mare (27 editions).

Literary activity
He made his literary debut in the literary review „Familia" with an article of the poet Şt. Augustin Doinaş, entitled *A voluptuous supporter of the image* (No.1, Jan. 1973)

Books published:

Poetry:
The Boundary Line Between the Words / Frontiera dintre cuvinte (1988);
Poems from the Middle-Age of the Room / Poeme din Ev-Mediul odăii (1991);
The Town Beneath The Whitewash Of The Walls / Oraşul de sub varul

pereţilor, (1994);
Treatise On the Blind Eye / Tratat despre Ochiul Orb (1996);
The Woman from the Middle-Age of the Room / Femeia din Ev-Mediul odăii (1996);
The Claw of the Letter / Gheara literei (1998);
The Agonizing Writing / Scrisul agonic (1999);
The North And Beyond The North / Nord, şi dincolo de Nord (2001);
The Nuptial Crags / Stânci nupţiale (2003);
Treatise On the Blind Eye / Traité sur l`Oeil Aveugle, (2004);
Monograms on the Stones of the North / Monograme pe Pietrele Nordului (2005);
Other Poems from the North / Alte poeme din Nord (2007);
Blind, through the North - Anthology / Orb, prin Nord – Antologie (2009);
Gold and Ivy / Aur şi Iederă (2011);
The North. A Gnosis of the Stone – Anthology / Nordul. O gnoză a pietrei – antologie (2011);
The grotto and the Letters / Grota şi literele (2013).
Black haze and calligraphy / Negură și caligrafie, 2014
The book from Satu Mare (anthology) / Cartea de la Satu Mare – antologie (2016).
The seal of the North / Sigiliul Nordului", (2016)
Maladiile lămpilor / The maladies of the lamps (2019)
Printre Vânătorii de orbi / Among the blind men chasers (2021)

Literary Criticism:
Saeculum. Metaphisics and Polemics, essay / *Saeculum. Metafizică şi polemică* (1995);
Culture and Literature in the lands of Satu Mare - A Dictionary covering the span between 1700 and 2000 / *Cultură şi literatură în ţinuturile Sătmarului. Dicţionar 1700-2000* (2000);
Annalist on the Frontier of Poesis, 1st volume / Cronicar pe Frontiera Poesis vol. I, 2007

Annalist on the Frontier of Poesis, 2nd volume / Cronicar pe Frontiera Poesis vol. II, 2012
Mihai Eminescu and the writers from Satu Mare (literary history)/ Mihai Eminescu și scriitorii sătmăreni (Documente de istorie literară, studii critice); coord. ediție, 2014;
The Ghilgames complex – essay on the subject of dust in the opera of Mihai Eminescu / „Complexul Ghilgameș" – Eseu despre motivul prafului în opera lui M. Eminescu, 2015.
The blindman in the poems of the light (essays) / „Orbul din poemele luminii, eseuri" (2016).
Lucian Blaga, Ipostazele „harfei de-ntuneric", 2020

Interviews:
Poesis. The Secret Shape of the Letter / Poesis. Conturul secret al literei (2009).

Bilingual editions:
Augenlieder, gedichte (translated by Christian W. Schenk and Simone Reicherts-Schenk, Germany, 1996);
Traité sur l'Oeil Aveugle (translated by Sabrina Russo, Montreal, 2004);
The North and beyond the North (translated by Olimpia Iacob, 2006);
Do severa I dalse od severa (translated into Serbian by Adam Puslojič and Miljurko Vukadinovič, Belgrad, 2007);
Versek (translated into Hungarian by Balázs Boróka, AB-art / Dellart, Limes 2010);
Other poems from the North (translated by Adam J. Sorkin and Olimpia Iacob, Iași, 2011).
*Gold and Ivy (*translated by Adam J. Sorkin and Olimpia Iacob), Eikon (2014*);*
*Ziemelu Aklais (*translated into Latvian by Leons Briedis), Omnia Mea, Riga, Latvia, 2014*;*
*Les pierres du Nord (*translated into French by Jean Poncet*),* Jacques Andre Editeur, Lyon, 2018;
Blinde augen weinen nicht, (translated into German by Christian W. Schenk), Dionysos, Germany, 2020.

www.ingramcontent.com/pod-product-compliance
Lightning Source LLC
Chambersburg PA
CBHW062112160726
48282CB00026B/772
* 9 7 8 9 3 8 8 3 1 9 7 5 1 *